So Many Questions

How to answer common questions about Christianity

by Simon Roberts

matthiasmedia

So Many Questions (revised edition)
© Matthias Media 2008

Matthias Media
(St Matthias Press Ltd ACN 067 558 365)
PO Box 225
Kingsford NSW 2032
Australia
Telephone: (02) 9663 1478; international: +61-2-9663-1478
Facsimile: (02) 9663 3265; international: +61-2-9663-3265
Email: info@matthiasmedia.com.au
Internet: www.matthiasmedia.com.au

Matthias Media (USA)
Telephone: 724 964 8152; international: +1-724-964-8152
Facsimile: 724 964 8166; international: +1-724-964-8166
Email: sales@matthiasmedia.com
Internet: www.matthiasmedia.com

ISBN 978 1 921068 93 5

Cover design and typesetting by Lankshear Design Pty Ltd.

Contents

About this course

Welcome to *So Many Questions*, a DVD-based training course on how to answer common questions about Christianity. By using this workbook and the accompanying DVD, you will learn some general principles for answering people's questions, as well as the specifics of how to answer 13 of the most frequently asked questions.

The course is divided into four main sections:

a. Introduction: This is comprised of four units which cover the general approach to answering people's questions.

b. Knowing: Some questions presume that the best answer is the one with the best evidence. To answer these types of questions, we need to present the evidence (either historical, scientific or philosophical) that supports our conclusion. This section answers four such questions.

c. Meaning: Other questions presume that either there is no such thing as 'the truth' or that we cannot know for sure what 'the truth' about God is. This section answers four questions that are based on the assumption that we can't know the truth.

d. Living: Finally, there are many questions concerned with how we ought to live. These questions seek to either understand or challenge the Bible's teaching on moral issues. The five questions in this section illustrate how these sorts of questions can be answered.

In total, there are 17 units to this course (4 introductory units and 13 answers to questions). The basic format of each unit is simple:

a. There are some starter questions which help you to start thinking about the main topic the unit will address.

b. You then watch the relevant segment of the DVD, taking notes in the space provided.

c. There are further questions to help you think about the topic in more depth and summarize the main points you would use in formulating an answer.

For each of the 13 questions, there are summaries along with suggestions for extra reading in Appendix 1. These can also be used as the basis for further discussion if you would like to explore a particular topic in more detail.

Different ways to use the course

As each unit is quite brief, there is considerable flexibility in how the course might be used. Here are some suggestions:

- An individual or couple could work through one unit per week as part of their personal Christian growth (say each Friday night or Sunday afternoon).
- A small Bible study group could do one unit each week during their regular meeting together (taking just 15-20 minutes each week).
- The units could be grouped together to yield more intensive courses of different lengths—for example, a nine-week course (two units per session = 40 minutes) or even a six-week course (three units per session = 60 minutes).
- Group leaders/coordinators could also choose not to cover all the questions. For example, you could choose the eight most common or relevant questions for the members of your group, and put them together in whatever combination you think is best.
- The course could also be run as a series of two or three Saturday morning seminars where six or nine units are completed at a time.

Contributors

We're very grateful to the following people, who gave of their time so generously in the filming of the DVD:

Chris Braga is the senior minister at Summer Hill Anglican Church.

Paul Grimmond is the Anglican chaplain of the University of New South Wales and senior minister at Unichurch.

Tony Payne is the Publishing Director at Matthias Media.

Claire Smith first trained as a nurse and is currently working on a PhD in New Testament studies. She ministers with her husband Rob at St Andrew's Cathedral, Sydney.

Al Stewart is the Anglican Bishop of the Wollongong region in Sydney.

In producing this course, our goal has been to equip Christians like you to answer people's questions wisely, graciously and compellingly. Our hope and prayer is that, as you do so, you will give glory to Christ by pointing people to him, and that, in his time and through his grace, many more might come to know him as their Lord.

Simon Roberts
January 2008

Introduction
Being prepared to give an account

There are two basic reasons why we need to know the answers to the various curly questions that are dealt with in this course.

Firstly, as Christians, these questions can bother us. Is the Bible really a reliable source of information? What about all the advances in science? Don't they somehow render our belief in God old-fashioned? And if God is so loving, why is there so much suffering in the world? At one time or another, these sorts of questions have passed through our minds as Christian believers. It is important that we know the answers to them. God is not afraid of the truth. By asking, researching and answering the questions that arise in our minds, we can only come to grasp his truth more fully.

Secondly, we, of course, need to know how to answer people who raise these questions with us. As both Peter and Paul remind us, being able to answer graciously and gently when we are called upon to do so is an important part of every Christian's relationship with 'outsiders' (as Paul calls them in Colossians 4:5-6; see also 1 Peter 3:15-16). In fact, answering questions is often the way we get into conversations with people about Christ and the gospel. As questions are raised (whether privately or around the lunch table at work), the way we react will either adorn the gospel and point the person towards Christ, or discredit Christ and reinforce people's prejudices against Christianity. It is important to be ready to answer well.

In the opening four units of this course, we'll discuss some general principles for answering questions about the Christian faith, before working through 13 very common questions which are asked about God and Christianity.

Think & discuss

Look through the list of common questions and challenges.

a. Tick the ones that have bothered you at some stage:
- ☐ How do I know God exists in the first place?
- ☐ Did Jesus really come back from the dead?
- ☐ Hasn't science disproved Christianity?
- ☐ You can't trust what the Bible says—it's been changed too much over the years!
- ☐ No-one can claim to have 'the truth'—everyone's opinion is valid.
- ☐ Wasn't Jesus just another great religious teacher?
- ☐ Discussing religion just divides people and causes problems!
- ☑ If the Bible is so clear, why can't Christians agree on what it says?
- ☐ Why is the Bible anti-gay?
- ☑ If God is good, why is there so much suffering in the world?
- ☑ Can't we just be good enough to please God?
- ☐ Christians are just a bunch of hypocrites!
- ☐ Do you have to go to church to be a Christian?

Le vd19 .
Roms:h1

b. Which ones have been you been asked by someone else? How would you rate the answer you gave?
- ☐ How do I know God exists in the first place?
- ☐ Did Jesus really come back from the dead?
- ☐ Hasn't science disproved Christianity?
- ☐ You can't trust what the Bible says—it's been changed too much over the years!
- ☐ No-one can claim to have 'the truth'—everyone's opinion is valid.
- ☐ Wasn't Jesus just another great religious teacher?
- ☐ Discussing religion just divides people and causes problems!
- ☐ If the Bible is so clear, why can't Christians agree on what it says?
- ☐ Why is the Bible anti-gay?
- ☐ If God is good, why is there so much suffering in the world?
- ☐ Can't we just be good enough to please God?
- ☐ Christians are just a bunch of hypocrites!
- ☐ Do you have to go to church to be a Christian?

Investigate

What do these passages tell us about why we ought to be ready to answer people when they ask us questions? What do they tell us about how we should answer questions?

Proverbs 15:14

1 Peter 3:14-16

Colossians 4:2-6

2 Timothy 2:22-26

📽 Watch & write: *Being prepared to give an account*

Now play the first introductory segment on the DVD, and take notes below. (NB. Throughout this course, space has been provided for you to take notes during the video segments. We strongly recommend that you do take notes, not just so that you can refer back to the material easily, but to aid your listening and recall. Taking notes is 'active listening'; it is harder work than 'passive listening', but much more effective.)

Peter says :-
-> Don't be fearful
-> Be ready to defend your faith
-> Be prepared
-> with gentleness/ respect - good conscience
   -> we would like to be listened to.
-> admit when we don't know
-> answering well is no guarantee that we'll be listened to.
-> PRAYER - for God's Holy Spirit

Pray

Conclude by praying for:
- a strong desire to be prepared to answer questions well, and the courage and confidence to take hold of opportunities when they arise
- people you know whose questions you may have to answer
- your own growth in knowledge and skills during this course.

Introduction
The art of listening

When we are asked a question (and particularly when we know the answer), it is tempting to jump in straight away with our reply. But this is rarely the best approach. In this section, we will explore how listening involves much more than just hearing the question being asked.

Think & discuss

Someone asks, "Why does God allow suffering?"

    a. What are some of the reasons a person might ask this question?

    b. How might these reasons affect the way you respond to this question?

Investigate

What do the following verses have to say about the importance of listening and understanding the reasons behind the questions that people ask?

Proverbs 18:2

Proverbs 17:27-28

Proverbs 20:5

 **Watch & write:** *The art of listening*

Pray

Conclude by praying for:

- wisdom and understanding as you seek to understand more about people and the questions they ask
- people you know whose questions you may have to answer.

Introduction
The art of answering

So we've been asked a question. We've listened carefully and have asked a question back to clarify what's really being asked, and we have listened to the person's response to see if we can discern if there is a question behind the question. But how do we go about answering?

Investigate

Read Acts 17:16-31.

1. What question is Paul asked?

2. How does Paul begin his answer (vv. 22-23)?

3. What does Paul say in the middle of his answer (vv. 24-29)?

4. What does Paul say at the end of his answer (vv. 30-31)?

Watch & write: *The art of answering*

Think & discuss

What helpful principles for answering questions can be drawn from Paul's speech to the men of Athens?

Pray

Conclude by praying for:
- clear thinking about God's word and world
- wisdom to know how to answer people's questions
- people you know whose questions you may have to answer.

Introduction
The art of follow-up

At the start of this course, we said that the goal is to win people, not arguments. Therefore the end of a conversation is not necessarily the end of our work. We ought to be looking for opportunities to follow up the discussion.

Think & discuss

1. After we have answered a person's question, what things can we do to make the most of that opportunity?

2. What can we do if we weren't able to answer their question very well?

 **Watch & write:** *The art of follow-up*

Pray

Conclude by praying for:
- opportunities to answer people's questions
- diligence to follow up people you have talked with
- people you know whose questions you may have answered already.

Question 1
How do I know God exists in the first place?

Think & discuss

1. What kind of question is this?
   A. Knowing
   B. Meaning
   C. Living

2. What are some of the reasons someone might have for asking this question?

3. How would you go about answering this question? Jot down the kinds of things you think could be included in an answer.

Watch & write

Before we play the first video answer, it is worth remembering that the answers on the DVD are not the only answers, nor do they convey every point that could be made. As discussed in 'The art of answering', there are often several ways to answer a question, and the best way will vary, depending on why the person is asking the question, what they already believe, and so on. These answers represent some of the main and important points which could be made, and they are given in the individual style and wording of the presenters. You need to work out how **you** would convey the answer to this question in your own words and personal style. This is the purpose of the final step of each unit (see below) where you summarize your own answer to the question.

Summarize your answer

In your own words, using three or four simple points, write down how you would answer the question "How do I know God exists in the first place?"

See page 77 for summary answers and further reading.

Question 2
Did Jesus really come back from the dead?

Think & discuss

1. What kind of question is this?
   A. Knowing
   B. Meaning
   C. Living

2. What are some of the reasons someone might have for asking this question?

3. How would you go about answering this question? Jot down the kinds of things you think could be included in an answer.

📽 Watch & write

Watch the video answer to question 2, and take notes in the space provided below.

Summarize your answer

In your own words, using three or four simple points, write down how you would answer the question "Did Jesus really come back from the dead?"

See page 77 for summary answers and further reading.

Question 3
Hasn't science disproved Christianity?

Think & discuss

1. What kind of question is this?
   A. Knowing
   B. Meaning
   C. Living

2. What are some of the reasons someone might have for asking this question?

3. How would you go about answering this question? Jot down the kinds of things you think could be included in an answer.

🎬 Watch & write

Watch the video answer to question 3, and take notes in the space provided below.

Summarize your answer

In your own words, using three or four simple points, write down how you would answer the question "Hasn't science disproved Christianity?"

See page 78 for summary answers and further reading.

Question 4

You can't trust what the Bible says—it's been changed too much over the years!

Think & discuss

1. What kind of question is this?
   - A. Knowing
   - B. Meaning
   - C. Living

2. What are some of the reasons someone might have for asking this question?

3. How would you go about answering this question? Jot down the kinds of things you think could be included in an answer.

Watch & write

Watch the video answer to question 4, and take notes in the space provided below.

Summarize your answer

In your own words, using three or four simple points, write down
how you would answer the question/challenge "You can't trust what
the Bible says—it's been changed too much over the years!"

See page 79 for summary answers and further reading.

Question 5

No-one can claim to have 'the truth'—everyone's opinion is valid

Think & discuss

1. What kind of question is this?
   A. Knowing
   B. Meaning
   C. Living

2. What are some of the reasons someone might have for asking this question?

3. How would you go about answering this question? Jot down the kinds of things you think could be included in an answer.

▤ Watch & write

Watch the video answer to question 5, and take notes in the space provided below.

Summarize your answer

In your own words, using three or four simple points, write down how you would answer the question/challenge "No-one can claim to have 'the truth'—everyone's opinion is valid".

See page 80 for summary answers and further reading.

Question 6

Wasn't Jesus just another great religious teacher?

Think & discuss

1. What kind of question is this?
   A. Knowing
   B. Meaning
   C. Living

2. What are some of the reasons someone might have for asking this question?

3. How would you go about answering this question? Jot down the kinds of things you think could be included in an answer.

▦ Watch & write

Watch the video answer to question 6, and take notes in the space provided below.

Summarize your answer

In your own words, using three or four simple points, write down how you would answer the question "Wasn't Jesus just another great religious teacher?"

See page 82 for summary answers and further reading.

Question 7
Discussing religion just divides people and causes problems!

Think & discuss

1. What kind of question is this?
   A. Knowing
   B. Meaning
   C. Living

2. What are some of the reasons someone might have for asking this question?

3. How would you go about answering this question? Jot down the kinds of things you think could be included in an answer.

■ Watch & write

Watch the video answer to question 7, and take notes in the space provided below.

Summarize your answer

In your own words, using three or four simple points, write down how you would answer the question/challenge "Discussing religion just divides people and causes problems!"

See page 83 for summary answers and further reading.

Question 8

If the Bible is so clear, why can't Christians agree on what it says?

Think & discuss

1. What kind of question is this?
   A. Knowing
   B. Meaning
   C. Living

2. What are some of the reasons someone might have for asking this question?

3. How would you go about answering this question? Jot down the kinds of things you think could be included in an answer.

◼ Watch & write

Watch the video answer to question 8, and take notes in the space provided below.

Summarize your answer

In your own words, using three or four simple points, write down how you would answer the question "If the Bible is so clear, why can't Christians agree on what it says?"

See page 84 for summary answers.

Question 9
Why is the Bible anti-gay?

Think & discuss

1. What kind of question is this?
   A. Knowing
   B. Meaning
   C. Living

2. What are some of the reasons someone might have for asking this question?

3. How would you go about answering this question? Jot down the kinds of things you think could be included in an answer.

▣ Watch & write

Watch the video answer to question 9, and take notes in the space provided below.

Summarize your answer

In your own words, using three or four simple points, write down how you would answer the question "Why is the Bible anti-gay?"

See page 85 for summary answers and further reading.

Question 10
If God is good, why is there so much suffering in the world?

Think & discuss

1. What kind of question is this?
    A. Knowing
    B. Meaning
    C. Living

2. What are some of the reasons someone might have for asking this question?

3. How would you go about answering this question? Jot down the kinds of things you think could be included in an answer.

▤ Watch & write

Watch the video answer to question 10, and take notes in the space provided below.

Summarize your answer

In your own words, using three or four simple points, write down how you would answer the question "If God is good, why is there so much suffering in the world?"

See page 86 for summary answers and further reading.

Question 11
Can't we just be good enough to please God?

Think & discuss

1. What kind of question is this?
   A. Knowing
   B. Meaning
   C. Living

2. What are some of the reasons someone might have for asking this question?

3. How would you go about answering this question? Jot down the kinds of things you think could be included in an answer.

▚ Watch & write

Watch the video answer to question 11, and take notes in the space provided below.

Summarize your answer

In your own words, using three or four simple points, write down
how you would answer the question "Can't we just be good enough to
please God?"

See page 87 for summary answers and further reading.

Question 12
Christians are just a bunch of hypocrites!

Think & discuss

1. What kind of question is this?
   A. Knowing
   B. Meaning
   C. Living

2. What are some of the reasons someone might have for asking this question?

3. How would you go about answering this question? Jot down the kinds of things you think could be included in an answer.

▦ Watch & write

Watch the video answer to question 12, and take notes in the space provided below.

Summarize your answer

In your own words, using three or four simple points, write down how you would answer the question/challenge "Christians are just a bunch of hypocrites!"

See page 88 for summary answers.

Question 13
Do you have to go to church to be a Christian?

Think & discuss

1. What kind of question is this?
   A. Knowing
   B. Meaning
   C. Living

2. What are some of the reasons someone might have for asking this question?

3. How would you go about answering this question? Jot down the kinds of things you think could be included in an answer.

🎬 Watch & write

Watch the video answer to question 13, and take notes in the space provided below.

Summarize your answer

In your own words, using three or four simple points, write down how you would answer the question "Do you have to go to church to be a Christian?"

See page 89 for summary answers and further reading.

Where to from here?

Well done! You should now be equipped to answer many of the common questions that people ask about Christianity. Even if you can't recall instantly how you would answer, say, question 3 ('Hasn't science disproved Christianity?'), we hope that you can now see that answering such a question is well within your reach. We hope that you have gained new confidence in discussing Christian things with your friends and family, and that God, in his kindness, will give you many opportunities to do so.

As noted in the introduction 'Being prepared to give an account', answering questions is often how we get into conversations with people about the gospel. Rarely does someone roll up to us and say, "Good sir, what must I do to be saved?" In addition, we do not always have the boldness or the opportunity to say to a friend, "Listen, how about I explain Christianity to you?" But questions do arise, and if we are confident enough to answer them, it can lead to actually sharing the content of the gospel with people.

To that end, a very useful next step would be to learn how to explain the gospel itself simply and clearly. The Matthias Media training course *Two Ways to Live: Know and share the gospel* is an excellent means of acquiring this skill. Sharpening your ability to explain the gospel will only add to your confidence in talking to others about your faith. Alternatively, doing the training course *Six Steps to Talking About Jesus* will also get you thinking about the practical steps you can take to start talking to your family and friends about the Lord Jesus. For more details, see the information at the back of this workbook, or visit the Matthias Media website (www.matthiasmedia.com.au).

May God give you his wisdom and courage as you do so.

Appendix 1
Answers and resources

1. How do I know God exists in the first place?

- We know God exists because of Jesus.
- We accept that Winston Churchill was Prime Minister of England during World War II because of the various historical records that exist. We may not have seen or heard him in person, but we trust the records. If asked, "Have you ever seen God?" we can reply, "No, but I might have if I'd been born at the right time".
- Jesus claimed to be God (e.g. John 5:18, 20:28-29), and his actions bore out that claim. If you'd been there, you would have seen and heard him. We weren't there, but the Gospels are the historical record of his life—what he did and said.
- Read a Gospel for yourself and check out his claims.
- If he is God, then you should serve him as God.

Further reading:
John Chapman, *A Fresh Start*, Matthias Media, Sydney, 1997, chapters 6-8.
Kel Richards, *Defending the Gospel*, Matthias Media, Sydney, 2006, chapter 2.

2. Did Jesus really come back from the dead?

- Firstly, if it didn't happen, everything Christianity stands for falls apart. Christianity is about much more than moral instruction.
- By and large, the New Testament was written to people who had already been persuaded that Jesus had been raised from the dead. Those close to the event were convinced that it had taken place.
- Jesus' tomb was empty. Jesus was executed and put into a tomb which was then guarded. But on the Sunday after his death, the tomb was found to be empty.

- After he rose, Jesus appeared to a whole range of people—even up to 500 people at one time (1 Cor 15:6). These appearances lasted 40 days and then stopped.
- A significant number of people who saw Jesus raised spent the rest of their lives on earth suffering persecution and loneliness, and travelling to the ends of the earth to tell people about Jesus. They were convinced that Jesus was alive. In turn, so many people were convinced by their testimony, Christianity spread rapidly throughout the Roman empire.

Other approaches:
- Some people want to dismiss the resurrection "because dead people don't rise". The problem with this view is that it assumes that dead people don't rise in order to prove that they don't. It not only leaves God out of the picture, it also assumes, by this logic, that nothing new can ever happen. We should examine the evidence instead of dismissing it in a close-minded way.

Further reading:
Peter Bolt, 'Questing for Jesus', *kategoria*, No. 8, 1998, pp. 9-31.

Frank Morrison, *Who Moved the Stone?*, Zondervan, Grand Rapids, 1987.

Kel Richards, *Defending the Gospel*, Matthias Media, Sydney, 2006, chapter 6.

3. Hasn't science disproved Christianity?
- The biblical God is the one who not only made the world but runs the world. God made the world to be an orderly place, so things usually run in a very normal way.
- God is not the explanation for things we otherwise couldn't explain. Because God is a God of good order, he is the reason that things can be explained by science. If the world was unpredictable, science would not be possible.
- Science cannot disprove God. In fact, inasmuch as science helps with the investigation of the past, it shows us how reliable the Bible is, and gives us good reasons for believing in Jesus Christ.

Other approaches:

- By this question, many people mean "Hasn't the theory of evolution replaced creation and so disproved Christianity?" They aren't usually talking about archaeology (which, incidentally, backs up the Bible at almost every point). Avoid a technical discussion about evolution, carbon dating, and so on. This usually gets nowhere. Ask what conclusion they are drawing from their evolutionary stance: Did the world come into being by chance? Or did God make the world using certain evolutionary processes? The answer to that will reveal the person's presuppositions about God's existence. How God made the universe is not as important a point as the fact that he made it. Steer the conversation towards talking about God's existence (see question 1) and talking about Jesus. If Jesus is God, it puts the creation/evolution debate in a new perspective. Encourage the person to find out if God exists and what he is like before tackling creation/evolution. Tell them to read a Gospel or a good book about Jesus.

Further reading:

Kirsten Birkett, *Unnatural Enemies*, Matthias Media, Sydney, 1997.

Kel Richards, *Defending the Gospel*, Matthias Media, Sydney, 2006, chapter 2.

4. You can't trust what the Bible says—it's been changed too much over the years!

- People often make this claim, but when you look at the evidence, you discover quickly that it is really a convenient modern fiction. The Bible won't be dismissed that easily.
- Behind the many different English translations we have today, there are the same Hebrew, Aramaic and Greek texts. This is why English translations are all so similar.
- We have many, many copies of the Old and New Testaments (over 5,000 manuscripts and fragments, in the case of the New Testament!) We have copies that are old and in good condition. They are often quite complete, coming from different locations and different branches of the church's history.

- By comparing these documents, it is very easy to spot when someone has changed the text (either accidentally or deliberately), and it is usually easy to correct those changes.
- We can also compare the Greek and Hebrew text to the many translations that were made into other languages, and the many quotations in other books and documents.
- There is too small a time lapse between when the Bible was written and the date of the earliest existing manuscripts; too many manuscripts for comparison with too much agreement and too few differences; and too much concern for accuracy in the transmission process for the claim that it has been changed to be true.

There is much more that can be said on this topic (for example, responses to objections that the Bible accounts were biased and inaccurate to begin with). An excellent book to both read and give away is *Is the New Testament History?* by Paul Barnett (Aquila Press, Sydney, 2003).

Further reading:
FF Bruce, *The Books and the Parchments*, Pickering & Inglis, Basingstoke, 1984.

Josh McDowell and Bill Wilson, *A Ready Defense: The Best of Josh McDowell*, Thomas Nelson, Nashville, 1993.

5. No-one can claim to have 'the truth'—everyone's opinion is valid.

- This is a very common view today. It is otherwise known as relativism, the claim that there is no such thing as objective or absolute truths which are true for everyone, whether or not they realize it. Instead, there is only subjective truth or 'what's true for me'-type truths.
- First, there's a logical inconsistency in the claim that there's no such thing as absolute truth because the claim itself is stating an absolute truth: "The truth is that there is no such thing as the truth".
- Second, there's a logical inconsistency in saying that all truth claims are equally valid because some truth claims are contradictory (e.g. Muslims deny that Jesus died and then rose from the dead. Christians say that he both died and rose. Both can't be true).

- Third, there's a moral inconsistency because relativism is unworkable. If there's no objective right and wrong, and each person decides their own truth and morality, how can one person judge or limit another person's actions? How can we say the Holocaust was wrong? How can we object to our car being stolen?
- The real question is "Is Jesus right?" Is he right when he says that he is the only one who can deal with people's sin? Is he right when he claims to be the only way people can be reconciled to God? And if Jesus is right, that's not arrogance or intolerance; that's truth everyone needs to hear.

Other approaches:

- The fact is that everyday people claim to have the truth about one thing or another. Everyone has a right to their own opinion. (It's no coincidence that freedom of speech is one of the great legacies of the Judeo-Christian heritage which lies behind modern western culture!) And Jesus taught that we ought to love everyone, and his life showed clearly that God's purposes are not brought about by force but by doing God's will. But Jesus was equally clear that he was the only one who could reconcile people to God. When it comes to our relationship with God, he even said, "Everyone who is of the truth listens to my voice" (John 18:37b). So Jesus not only claimed to have the truth, he claimed he was the only way to God and that all other paths lead people in the wrong direction (John 14:6). Simply having an opinion about Jesus doesn't make you right; you need to ask if your opinion is based on an open-minded examination of the facts. When was the last time you read one of the Gospels?

Further reading:

John Dickson, *If I were God, I'd make myself clearer*, Matthias Media, Sydney, 2002.

Josh McDowell and Bill Wilson, *A Ready Defense: The Best of Josh McDowell*, Thomas Nelson, Nashville, 1993.

Kel Richards, *Defending the Gospel*, Matthias Media, Sydney, 2006, chapters 7 and 8.

Fritz Ridenour, *So What's the Difference?*, Regal Books, Ventura, 1967.

James Sire, *Chris Chrisman goes to College*, IVP, Downers Grove, 1993.

6. Wasn't Jesus just another great religious teacher?

- We love to think of Jesus as just a religious teacher because that way we can domesticate him. But the real Jesus won't be put in a box that easily.
- Why was Jesus crucified? Jesus healed people, he said 'love your neighbour' and he fed crowds of people. The religious authorities didn't crucify him for any of these; they crucified him because he claimed to be God's king. Furthermore, he claimed to be God come in the flesh. He claimed that every human being must serve or worship him, that his death is a great sacrifice in our place, and that trusting him is the only way to find forgiveness and avoid hell. He also claimed that he will be the final judge on judgement day.
- These aren't just the claims of a great religious teacher. Jesus is either a very bad man who lied and deceived people, or he is mad and ought to be locked up. Or he is who he claimed to be.
- Jesus demonstrated that he was, in fact, God's great king when he died and rose again. He defeated death and was raised to new life as the ruler of the world.

Other approaches:
- Ask who they are comparing to Jesus, and then compare the claims of those teachers. Jesus claimed that he came to reveal God and rescue people from sin. Others may claim to reveal God (although many don't) but only Jesus claims to rescue from sin. The claims of various religious teachers are so different, they can't just be lumped together, and the evidence to show that Jesus is who he said he is far exceeds that of other religious teachers.

Further reading:
Kel Richards, *Defending the Gospel*, Matthias Media, Sydney, 2006, chapter 5.

Fritz Ridenour, *So What's the Difference?*, Regal Books, Ventura, 1967.

7. Discussing religion just divides people and causes problems!

- Well, maybe it does, but what's so bad about that? When we discuss important issues, people always have differences of opinion. We disagree about politics, the environment and education; should we just stop talking to each other so that we never disagree?
- Most of us would agree that important questions have to be raised, even if they do cause division. Why? Because when there are issues of truth, issues of justice, and issues of right and wrong, division matters.
- Very often when we say "Discussing religion just divides people and causes problems", what we actually mean is that religion is a private matter and that people can believe whatever they like. There is no point discussing religion because it's just my opinion versus your opinion.
- Jesus came and taught and lived and died and rose again so that everyone can be forgiven and come to know God. If that is true, it matters. If it isn't true, then that matters too. But surely Jesus is just too important to leave on the shelf gathering dust. He is too important *not* to talk about—even if he does cause division.

Other approaches:

- The real issue is not that we discuss religion too much; we actually discuss religion too little. More to the point, we want to leave God out of the picture and keep him at a comfortable distance from our day-to-day lives. But that is the root cause of all our problems. We try to live life as if God weren't there, but we not only make a mess of our own lives, we also make a mess of the lives of others and the world around us. Because we have rejected and rebelled against God, we are under his judgement. That's why we need Jesus. He is the only way we can escape that judgement, and receive new and eternal life.

Further reading:

Don Carson, *The Gagging of God*, Zondervan, Grand Rapids, 1996.
(For advanced readers.)

8. If the Bible is so clear, why can't Christians agree on what it says?

- Christians do disagree on some things, but the reality is that, for millions of Christians, there is an incredibly high level of agreement about what the Bible says.
- What the Bible teaches about God, the problem of human rebellion against God, the reality of judgement, that Jesus is both the Christ and God come in the flesh, the central place of Jesus' death and resurrection, what it means to receive new life through him—these are all areas where Christians everywhere stand together.
- There are also differences, but this does not mean that the Bible is unclear. The vast majority of the time, the Bible is no more difficult to understand than the daily newspaper.
- Very often disagreements come about because people have stopped listening to the Bible and are paying more attention to their own opinions, their particular group's traditions or what they feel is right. In those cases, the disagreements are not because the Bible is unclear, but because people are ignoring what it says and are concentrating on something else.

Other approaches:

- When Christians say that the Bible is clear, we don't mean that every part of the Bible is equally clear. Not every sentence or paragraph is simple. But the central themes are very clear: God, sin, judgment, salvation only being possible because of God's mercy, who Jesus is and the significance of what he did, and so on. These topics are addressed often and consistently.
- When Christians say that the Bible is clear, we don't mean that it makes clear to us everything we want to know. The Bible is silent on many questions we might have, or it only provides partial information. But the Bible *does* contain everything we need to know God truly, and to know how we ought to relate to him and please him.

9. Why is the Bible anti-gay?

- We used to live in a society that would say, "I disapprove of what you say, but I will defend to the death your right to say it". Today, saying "I disagree with you" is often taken to mean that I am intent on doing you physical violence, and saying "I love you" is often taken to mean "I agree with everything you have to say". But reality is more complex than that.

- Both the Old and New Testaments are clear and unambiguous: sexual activity between a man and a man, or between a woman and a woman, is wrong.

- This is not just some arbitrary rule. The rule is there because God planned sex for a marriage relationship—that is, a lifelong union between a man and a woman. The purpose of this good gift within marriage is for the husband and the wife to bond to one another, to enjoy each other and to give to one another. Sex is also the way that God has chosen to bring children into the world: he wants them to be born in the context of committed and loving relationships.

- That is why the Bible is against any form of sex outside of marriage—heterosexual *and* homosexual. The Bible is not anti-gay. Homosexual activity is no better or worse than any other sin; it is just one of the many ways every single person in our world says "no" to God. The solution we *all* need is Jesus' death on the cross for us.

Other *approaches:*

- Are some sexual practices wrong? For instance, do you think that paedophilia is a natural and right way to behave? How, then, do we make a judgement about any particular sexual practice? By majority opinion? If that were so, the earth was flat in the 16th century, Hitler was right in late 1930s Germany, and homosexuality was wrong about 20 years ago. In the end, only the creator of the world has the right (and the wisdom) to declare something right or wrong. Only he has the authority, and only he has the complete picture. If we accept who Jesus is (thereby accepting God's authority over the world), we must listen to him, and he clearly says that engaging in homosexual practice is not the way he created us to behave. It goes against the created order. Even so, Christians don't hate homosexuals. We want to be kind and accepting of them. We want to help them work through their struggles.

Further reading

Michael Hill, *The How and Why of Love: An Introduction to Evangelical Ethics*, Matthias Media, Sydney, 2002, chapters 9 and 11.

Christopher Keane (ed.), *What Some of You Were: Stories about Christians and homosexuality*, Matthias Media, Sydney, 2001.

Thomas E Schmidt, *Straight & Narrow?: Compassion & Clarity in the Homosexuality Debate*, IVP, Downers Grove, 1995.

10. If God is good, why is there so much suffering in the world?

- The problem of suffering is one of the hardest questions we face as human beings. It is interesting that the Bible is not scared of the problem. In the Bible, you see people trying to reconcile their knowledge that God is good and is in control of everything with their own experiences of suffering, and succeeding.
- The Bible is very clear that God is both all-loving and all-powerful—that he's completely good and completely in control. So why doesn't he fix things and stop bad things happening?
- It's because God is giving us what we chose. Even though God's original creation was very good (a place of peace, safety and prosperity), human beings rejected his kingship over creation and over us, and so we not only earned ourselves his eternal wrath, we also brought pain and death and suffering into the world.
- Some suffering is just part of life 'post-Genesis 3' (like the man born blind in John 9). However, some suffering is the end result of a particular sin (e.g. Rom 1:18-32) and some suffering is the direct judgement of God on sin (e.g. the lame man in John 5:1-14).
- Suffering is not a problem that God looks at from a distance. He doesn't leave us to solve it. Suffering is what God himself did to solve our problem. The cross is where we see that God is all-loving and

all-good: while we were still sinners, Christ died for us. And the cross is where we see that God is all-powerful: what we were powerless to do (i.e. save ourselves from God's wrath—the wrath we deserved), Christ did for us. Jesus secured the victory that offers hope to us all in a new and perfect creation, free from all the ugliness of this world.

Further reading:

Don Carson, How Long, O Lord?, Baker, Grand Rapids, 1991.

John Dickson, If I were God, I'd end all the pain, Matthias Media, Sydney, 2001.

Paul E Little, How to Give Away Your Faith, IVP, Downers Grove, 1988, chapter 5.

Kel Richards, Defending the Gospel, Matthias Media, Sydney, 2006, chapter 8.

11. Can't we just be good enough to please God?

- The problem is that we don't live good lives. If we are honest, we don't live up to our own moral codes. We don't always have a clear conscience. And if we don't live up to our own moral code, how will we go at living up to God's standards?

- Jesus summarized what God wants of us into two commandments. The second of the commandments is to love our neighbour as we love ourselves. Jesus says your neighbour is everyone, including your enemies. How many people love their enemies?

- But then, for most people, it gets even worse, because he says that's not even the great commandment. The really big commandment is that we are to love God with all our heart, all our mind, all our soul and all our strength. God has to occupy first place in our life. But we all ignore God, and very often we reject him outright.

- If we could really be good enough to please God, why did Jesus die? The cross would have been unnecessary. Jesus himself, on the night before he died, prayed to his Father that, if there was any other way other than him dying, God might make it happen. But there was no other way to save us. Relying on Jesus' death on our behalf is the only way to be acceptable to God.

Other approaches:

* There are two issues here. One is that we aren't good. We all reject and ignore God, and fail to love those around us. But secondly, we can't repay the debt we owe or ward off the judgement we deserve simply by doing the good that is expected of us as God's creatures. Doing good does not build up a positive balance in some divine bank account that can offset the bad things we do (just like we can't avoid a fine for exceeding the speed limit because, on other occasions, we travel below the speed limit). That's why we need Jesus—both to face judgement in our place (so that we don't have to) and to change us (so that we can begin to live a genuinely good life).

Further reading:

John Chapman, *A Fresh Start*, Matthias Media, Sydney, 1997, chapter 11.

Kel Richards, *Defending the Gospel*, Matthias Media, Sydney, 2006, chapter 3.

12. Christians are just a bunch of hypocrites!

* To write off all Christians as hypocrites may be an easy excuse for ignoring Christianity, but it's hardly fair.
* Sure, there are, no doubt, some people who pretend to be Christians—people who are not serious about Jesus but who play the part so that others see them and think that they are Christians. But the vast majority of professing, Bible-believing Christians are genuinely following Jesus—genuinely seeking to live life his way.
* Having said that, at another level, Christians don't live the perfect life that Jesus lived. Christians fail to live the life we want to live. But Christians are usually very open about this; they don't pretend to be something they are not because they know that they are not the people they want to be. They are honest about that.
* Christians try to love and forgive because God has loved and forgiven them. We don't always get it right, and each day we come and pray to God that he'll keep forgiving us, and that he'll help us to love and forgive others. That's not hypocrisy; that's honesty. I need help. Don't you?

Other approaches:

- This question often relates to certain practices by Christians throughout history, such as the abuse of children by priests, alleged mistreatment of indigenous people by Christian missionaries, and so on. We don't want to trivialize wrong behaviour. People should be held responsible for their actions, and this should especially be so in the case of Christian leaders and teachers. But the crimes of the few can't be used to dismiss Jesus or the great good that the majority of Christians do. Christians claim to be sinful and in need of help. It is not hypocritical for us to err, for that is part of the fabric of our belief that we are rebels at heart and that we will continue to make mistakes. Christianity is about forgiveness, not perfect performance.
- It is not really fair to judge the truth of Jesus (who he was, what he did) by the bad behaviour of some who claim to be his followers. Jesus himself indicated that, in the future, many people would claim to bear his name but actually know nothing of him. When some of these people commit atrocities in his name, it is hardly Jesus' fault! Nor does this have any bearing on whether you are going to accept Jesus' claim over your life. Those who do wrong will have to give account to God for their actions. And so will you.

13. Do you have to go to church to be a Christian?

- If you want to understand whether you need to go to church to be a Christian, you need to understand what a Christian is first.
- A Christian is someone who has turned from living for themselves to living with Jesus as their King and Saviour. Jesus has rescued them from their sin, and brought them forgiveness. He's the one who sets the direction of a Christian's life. But being Christian is not a solo thing or a spectator sport. Being Christian is about being part of God's people. It's about being part of a team. That's where church comes in.
- Church is not a building or an event you 'attend'; church is a group of Christians gathering together to have the Bible taught

to them as a group so that they'll know how to behave with each other as a group. They go to pray with each other and for each other, and they go to encourage each other. This is because being a Christian is not just about my relationship with God; it's also about how I relate to the rest of Jesus' people.

- If you are a Christian and you choose not to go to church, ultimately you're denying that Jesus is in charge of your life. It's like getting married and then not living with your wife or husband, or saying that you are committed to the sports team but not showing up for training or matches.

Other approaches:
- Find out why the person doesn't like the idea of church and when they last went to church. It may well be that they have a specific negative past experience or a misconception. Or it could be that they don't want to commit their lives to what God thinks is best. Clarify what church is about, but also invite them along to church so that they can experience firsthand what a loving Christian community is like.

Further reading:
Kel Richards, *Defending the Gospel*, Matthias Media, Sydney, 2006, chapter 8.

Matthias Media is a ministry team of like-minded, evangelical Christians working together to achieve a particular goal, as summarized in our mission statement:

To serve our Lord Jesus Christ, and the growth of his gospel in the world, by producing and delivering high quality, Bible-based resources.

It was in 1988 that we first started pursuing this mission together, and in God's kindness we now have more than 250 different ministry resources being distributed all over the world. These resources range from Bible studies and books, through to training courses and audio sermons.

To find out more about our large range of very useful products, and to access samples and free downloads, visit our website:

www.matthiasmedia.com.au

How to buy our resources

1. Direct from us over the internet:
   – in the US: www.matthiasmedia.com
   – in Australia and the rest of the world: www.matthiasmedia.com.au

2. Direct from us by phone:
   – in the US: 1 866 407 4530
   – in Australia: 1800 814 360 (Sydney: 9663 1478)
   – international: +61-2-9663-1478

3. Through a range of outlets in various parts of the world. Visit **www.matthiasmedia.com.au/international.php** for details about recommended retailers in your part of the world, including www.thegoodbook.co.uk in the United Kingdom.

4. Trade enquiries can be addressed to:
   – in the US: sales@matthiasmedia.com
   – in the UK: sales@ivpbooks.com
   – in Australia and the rest of the world: sales@matthiasmedia.com.au

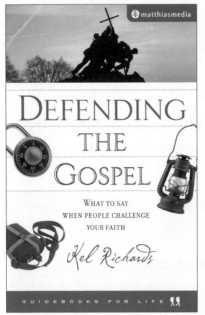

Six Steps to Talking About Jesus

By Simon Roberts and Simon Manchester

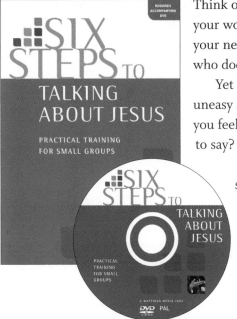

Think of the people around you: your family, your workmates, the man at the newsagency, your neighbours. Is there a single one of them who doesn't need to be following Jesus?

Yet like so many Christians, do you feel uneasy about reaching out to people? Perhaps you feel unsure about where to start and what to say?

Six Steps to Talking about Jesus is a short course that goes back to square one, and helps you make a start. Over 6 interactive sessions you'll look at:

- the core motivation for reaching out to others
- how to depend on God in prayer
- how to invite people to read a book or come to an event
- how to tell your own story of what God has done for you in Christ
- how to explain the gospel of Jesus in a simple way.

This is a course designed to be done in a small group context, and does not require an 'expert leader'. It is ideal preparation for a church mission.

To run the course you will need:

- a workbook for each person, which also contains notes for group leaders
- a DVD to use in the group.

FOR MORE INFORMATION OR TO ORDER CONTACT:

Matthias Media
Telephone: +61-2-9663-1478
Facsimile: +61-2-9663-3265
Email: info@matthiasmedia.com.au
Internet: www.matthiasmedia.com.au

Matthias Media (USA)
Telephone: 1-866-407-4530
Facsimile: 724-964-8166
Email: sales@matthiasmedia.com
Internet: www.matthiasmedia.com

Where to, Lord?

6 studies on guidance for small groups and individuals

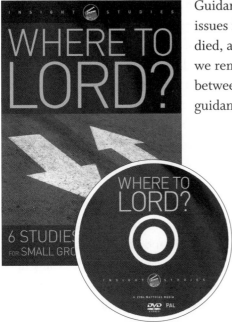

Guidance can be one of the most frustrating issues for Christians. We know that Jesus has died, and that heaven lies in the future. But we remain unsure about everything in between. We have many questions about guidance, such as:

- How does God guide his people today?
- What does God want me to do with my life?
- Where does he want me to work?
- Who does he want me to marry?
- How can I know God's will for my life?
- Am I missing out on God's personal guidance?
- How do I hear his voice?

These 6 studies on guidance will help you plot a course through these difficult issues.

Where to, Lord? is part of our Insight Studies series, which uses a mix of Bible investigation, group discussion and video input to help you interact with God's word. Perfect for groups looking for a refreshing change, the studies and DVD format are specifically designed to work together to enable any group to put together the pieces on difficult topics such as guidance and holiness.

FOR MORE INFORMATION OR TO ORDER CONTACT:

Matthias Media
Telephone: +61-2-9663-1478
Facsimile: +61-2-9663-3265
Email: info@matthiasmedia.com.au
Internet: www.matthiasmedia.com.au

Matthias Media (USA)
Telephone: 1-866-407-4530
Facsimile: 724-964-8166
Email: sales@matthiasmedia.com
Internet: www.matthiasmedia.com

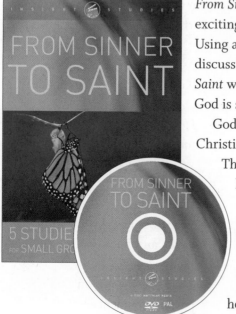